Homesick

For all those that have a home beyond Earth

Merasen-na Jamir

ISBN 978-93-5610-248-4
© Merasen-na Jamir 2022
Published in India 2022 by Pencil

Contributors:
Illustrator: Syn Ltr

A brand of
One Point Six Technologies Pvt. Ltd.
123, Building J2, Shram Seva Premises,
Wadala Truck Terminal, Wadala (E)
Mumbai 400037, Maharashtra, INDIA
E connect@thepencilapp.com
W www.thepencilapp.com

Author biography

Merasen-na Jamir is a twenty three year old hailing from Dimapur, Nagaland, India. She is pursuing her Msc in Counselling Pyschology and tries to connect one's state of mind with her writings. *Homesick* is her second poetry book through which she wishes to build a secret bond with her readers. She previously wrote *Paper Boats,* her first poetry book and is also the author of the novella, *Into My Abyss*Abyss.

CONTENTS

We leave trails of what we bleed

Everyone that has mourned knows it's colder on those days.

When you see your shadow but you can only see them.

Some people care on some days, and don't when you need it the most.

You begin to think will my laughter change without them?

Will the love I had be the same or will it grow bitter?

What more can you do after they already leave?

You sit there watching their graves half built,

Can you put down all those flowers with grace?

On a chilly day when the Sun decides to hide,

Drizzles of rain begin to accompany you.

Slowly, you have to stand up and begin to move,

And we will leave trails of what we bleed.

Meet me half way up the hill

I will quietly walk without my footsteps being heard,

I will see the yellow waffle house and not care to stop.

Lilies on my hand from a random flower shop on the gram.

Shall I pick up a cup of coffee with extra cream, because you love it that way?

Father, I don't want to stop. You know I cannot move ahead like that.

It is faith that is leading me, strength from your foundation.

You told me, come all those that are thristy.

Father, am I thristy? I cannot tell, my feet is in pain.

If I decide to take a deep breath and then run as fast as I can,

Will that stop my eyes from forming tears and crying all the way?

When I walk up the hill, will the flowers be withered or will I see the coming of spring?

I have never been one to walk, but I will climb.

So meet me half way up the hill when I decide to stop after all my tries.

Touch me and your skin will burn

Heaven must have told you wonders, but did it tell you about me?

I am not a mixture of light and darkness like you assume,

The sun is on borrowed light, the moon it's distant cousin.

If you could catch a falling star and make a wish, would you?

Or would the fear from tearing your hands apart hold you back?

Shooting stars are falling stars and falling stars are dead stars,

So would I wish it to come back to life and live inside my eyes?

I have been carved in a form you can see and feel, so you decide to do as you please.

Touch me in between my thighs and rub my breasts,

When I scream you hear sounds of hallelujah and break me.

But don't you know I am not screaming for safety?

I am yelling for your humanity leaving your soul.

Haven't I asked before, *Have you heard from Heaven about me?*

Touch me and your skin will burn.

Repent before the sand stops

I have a fountain of never ending warmth in me that lets kindness rests.

Had I let it run dry, you would tell me how much it hurts when your tongue falls off your mouth.

How would you? Would you paint it by the blood gushing out?

But your fingers will be nailed one at a time to the floor.

Would you show me with the tears in your eyes or would it burst because your eyelids are stitched up together?

Grandma told me, being wise is a burden too heavy to carry.

What would happen if I decide I don't want to carry yours anymore?

I forgave you when you blamed it on the liquor.

But will I forgive you for your lies?

There is a God I believe in, and if you do too,

Go to Him and pray.

Homicide

I will tell you of all the ones I tried to kill.

Without remorse or any sense of conscious.

I bet all we wanted was a little relief.

When all ways are blocked and you give up being lost,

How many did you kill inside your head?

And how many times did you kill yourself there?

In how many ways have you thought of pulling the end?

How many ideas have you pulled together to make sure it doesn't hurt as much as you are hurting?

We are murderous on the run.

Trying to save so many yet none of our own.

That's the irony because they call you an angel right?

When you are but a hypocrite, trying to stop these homocides.

The days we don't count

I make my coffee in the morning just to drain it down the sink because I forgot to drink it while it was warm.

I buy myself some pizza just to eat a slice and leave it in the fridge till I throw it out.

I tell myself that my mind is blank but it hurts from the crowd inside there.

Somedays are odd like that. But I will roll out my extension cord and place it beside my bed.

I will charge my waterbag and warm my legs after.

I sip the tea I did not ask Mum to make for me.

I will lay down on my pillow and begin to write,

because this is why I write poetry.

To write about the things that nobody talks about because it's an unusually normal thing.

But I will write about it, and you will read it and we will all feel better together.

Probably a fourth grader poem

I always thought I should have been a tree when I was a child.

In fourth grade I thought they smiled each time they moved as I walked passed by.

When I was a teenager, I was wondered if it was innocence or just stupidity.

Turns out, I was better off as a tree.

Cut me down, but do it in front of me.

Show me your insincerity for providing you too much all these years.

Make a bench out of me, a table to place your food, burn the rest of me to ashes.

These humans do things even the devil would plead to stop.

These humans do things that aren't in the storyline.

These humans makes a human like me to wish to be a tree.

Even tragedy can be art

So you kissed my lips and I had to break brushes.

Can I beg for a new one if I wash it with my vomit?

How many times did I glorify you in my poems?

How many tragedies did I remake into art?

5000 ways for you 5-4-3-2-1 slaps, I carried this.

Forgiveness comes easy when you don't ask for it.

My Tee Shirt burnt because you wrote on it.

My hands type because you started this.

You dont end wars when the other did not even enter the battlefield.

I talk to God about You

I wonder what He thinks, when He sees me cry.

If it hurts me for the thousanth time,

Will you bury me for the thousand and one time?

I walk like the way berries smell even when I am rotting.

Carrying a pile of two thousand corpses they killed.

Hunt me down like I came down here just to be hunted.

Haunt me like I was born to be possessed.

If this is just what I have to carry to become the tunnel,

Do you think there will be light when you walk through?

You don't think I cry myself to sleep when you come to enslave me?

I fool around and make mistakes too, but never towards you.

So when I talk to God about You, He knows You.

Robbers they come and go

When I decide to run, you want me to be bare so I can feel the ground,

The Earth does not want to harm me, you do.

When all nations begged me to stay, I chose you.

I waved your flag but you wore your gloves to point at me.

Told the gaurds to let me become skin and bones,

In your dungeon filled with skulls of all those you robbed,

You forgot I too can write another Robinhood story.

One that will exile you for your betrayal.

The same bones you want me to become,

Will be the bones that tear these bars-

Till I get to you.

They do not want you

The body of my poem, they have grown tired of you.

Weary and disgusted, it echoes for your name to be erased.

They do not want praises in your stead.

They no longer welcome you here.

Patiently waiting for the day you wash ashore,

Far away from the sea of my poetry.

Red sweater and grey pyjama

I remember seeing two willow trees about three feet apart from each other.

The leaves, they fell but were green not orange.

Did I drink red tea or ate some dumplings?

I don't remember the events of that day anymore.

Yet the smell of all the people still lingers.

I laughed even when my chest felt heavy.

Maybe you remember the days when you felt joy in the middle of misery.

All the colours I saw were more than what the rainbow held.

Even on rainy days, I hope I remember that day.

When all else was black and white,

I was a happy girl in my red sweater and grey pyjama.

He will meet me by the river

If I have a shovel, he will have a car on standby.

He told me to dig up all the bodies I never wanted to bury.

Carry them with you for they are yours.

Corpses will only haunt you every night.

He told me to freely let go without strings attached,

Never stay in a place where there is no sunshine just because it doesn't bring rain.

I will build my body with bricks and he will tell me to put it down.

These storms cannot break you, when you are with you.

These storms will not touch you, when I am the storm.

When he goes away, he will wait by the river for me.

The fireflies we saw that summer

My eyes saw a colour of one that words cannot form.

Walking on the side of that almost dry paddy fields,

The grass makes everything itch but my mind denies,

The girls walking ahead of me sang a familiar tune.

I used to know that song, I think.

The sound of the utensils, a mother calling her son for dinner,

Little huts that bring warmth to these homes.

Will I ever feel what I felt when I was young?

Running as fast as I can to surrender myself on top of the dried hay.

Can I run when I am almost out of breath, when the old man comes shouting?

But when we stopped by between the two lakes we assumed to be haunted and creepy,

The fireflies glowed differently in that eerie darkness.

And we were once again reminded why the dark is necessary for the light.

23

The old man we all love

I cannot write the word *loved,* because even when you are gone, you still remain.

Even with your more than skin deep illness, the weight of your complain was lighter than any feather we carried.

If grace had a name, maybe it was yours.

Someone told us, even when people die, death cannot conquer names.

So, it is yours obü.

You were the man who wanted to help even when you were the one who needed a hand the most.

You carried your cross beautifully and never stopped even when you were weary.

I know, you did not feel love from some souls that left you abandoned,

But your sister mourned for you the way angels would have.

Time and again, life has only taught me that the good ones depart first.

You are the man who made me feel like I had my grandfather all along.

I cannot thank you enough and we owe you too much for this life.

Maybe the place you are at now is where we are *homesick* for.

All the eleven eleven I wasted on you

If I had a talk with the genie, I would tell him

You can take back all those wishes I made on you.

I should have prayed about not learning about loving myself from you.

That it didn't take eleven rolls of tissue to know heartbreak.

I wonder what was it that I was mourning for?

All the lies you painted in pink while love is red?

Where does this bitterness comes from, they ask me.

It is not from the scars of what he gave me to fight,

It is from the all the ways I cannot forgive myself

For placing a killer first before a wounded healer.

It took me nine hundred mistakes for the number itself to wish a wish for me.

If they don't love you

Come to me and taste my poetry,

Pour it over all the holes they dug.

Who told you that your body was a basement?

Do not store their trauma, do not keep their traits.

What they built is made of sand, it will be washed.

You are not what they told you you were.

You shall never become what they are.

Suck up all the nectar from my letters,

Make them dance around your wounds,

So when you recover, you only carry words that heal.

I am losing places

I don't have a definite place now.

These funeral homes I go to seem to take something from me.

A piece of them and a piece of me.

My heart is becoming a place for sharp edges.

You made me feel love and taught me love, and then you left,

How the fuck am I suppose to beat that while I am still here?

If I scream and kneel before your grave for days will you give it back to me?

When your pain ended, mine began.

How am I suppose to give people homes, when I am losing all of mine to stay?

I am losing places, somedays too many at a time.

Tell the angels you meet up there not to hurry you home.

I pretend to understand poetry

I sit under the moonlight to ask, *what am I?*

I have all the stars build a galaxy inside me and still have room for more,

But I do not understand poetry.

It is a language I speak fluenty but still foreign to me.

Because a lot of you has passed before me, before I existed.

And all that beauty that I missed, how will I cover up that loss?

How will I understand poetry when I cannot meet you all?

I am the sculptor but you are my chosen clay.

Grief told me a story

The only mercy grief has shown me is that I am capable of loving.

To have the opportunity to hold someone precious is something many a lot miss.

Why would you choose that?

How light is your heart when you do not feel the loss of a life enough to break?

Don't you think it is lovely that we have so much to worry over?

To be given the honour to acknowledge what loss really means

Grief told me a story,

Real grief is one when you cannot feel it.

You are your own letter

The truth is, some things are better kept hidden.

So that they are precious and only belong to you.

Maybe this is why, regardless of the languages that exist

You sometimes cannot explain what you feel.

How to befriend yourself

So you get lonely when you alone can feel it.

The reason why some things cannot be explained,

Why certain pain can only be felt and not said,

Is so that you can figure it out on your own,

To let you realize that only you are the stamp that can fit your letter.

The lonliness is just a disguise for you to find that.

The letter M

But when I met her, it was like all of the ruined friendships assembling to piece up.

As if betrayal itself bowed in repentance.

Glazed with mercy and a basket full of concern,

I wonder if this is what it feels like when I love other people,

For many a times people have only loved me for what I give.

I haven't seen her yet so I wonder what the colour of her eyes looks like,

If her long hair is as strong as I think it is, so she can save someone jumping off a building.

I believe her ears carry pillows because they seem to always hear my conversations and store them.

I want her to be a poetry that can dance around my pages,

Romanticize friendships because a lot of us carry broken ones.

And when they ask me who taught me this, I would say *"The letter M"*.

When I go to the market

I will wear a yellow sun dress filled with daises,

Something I have never worn before.

With a dusty slingback wedge and a hobo bag.

I hope I smell some freshly baked treats from all the bakeries I cross.

My hair in a fishtail, I hope the sun will be kind.

As I walk through the market, I will look at all the people.

You may be gone for a little while now, but I hope I see you.

Admist the crowd a similar face to yours, almost familiar,

I hope it glances at me, this stranger and smile to me in hugs.

I do not know mercy in my poetry

Sink with me for I am cruel.

Bathe with me in the blood of my characters,

As I finish them one by one, cry for them.

I am a torturer who loves safety and comfort.

Sufferings in the sufferings I give you.

I have a terminal illness you see,

To kill all those that live of inside me.

Slowly transferring my beloved ones to you.

The boy who wears Mary Jane shoes

Down the half dusty, half cement road you can turn right

There is an alley filled with cats that a boy feeds.

Empty cans of tuna and some carton of milk.

This I know because after he leaves, I clean the trash he forgets.

I watch him with the binoculars I stole from a little fellow.

I thought I could used it better than him.

Beige turtle neck with a worn out brown coat,

A faded indigo blue pants, this boy wears.

If I am a thief, I would love to rob some of the kindness of the boy who wears Mary Jane shoes.

The secret to happiness

I will find my lover who will love me for all my shallow parts.

I shall witness his bravery to love me after seeing it all,

But try as he may, he would not understand my entirety.

I am not disappointed my love,

I walked on thin ice my whole life and have grown tired of fear.

To ask a human to read me over and over is too much a price.

I will pull out all of my hair from my head, tear myself limb by limb,

But I shall not hold another part of me captive.

Set every unexplainable portion of me free,

We shall all dance to this happiness of coming in terms with the unknown.

I met this writer CB

I tried painting this poet with my brush,

Because she wrote me love letters every single day.

So bare and naked, so delicate, I could trace her heart.

Where every drop of blood flows and how her organs ache.

I have seen a garden grow with little dandelions and tulips.

I have witnessed a thousand wonders in this life so far,

Yet I have only just understood that you don't wear courage.

You become it.

So I painted this poet with my colours,

But none justified to the words she wrote to me.

I met this writer CB and she smells like poetry in human verse.

The ones you need to be wary of

It's the ones that pretend to read books that spits more venom.

The ones that dont want to fit in the crowd rather than not fitting in.

The ones that deliberately tell you so much about life.

Everybody will stare but not to glorify them.

See their eyes of wariness, know that the atmosphere is a warning signal.

It's the ones with the handerchiefs that reminds you of babies you need to stay away from.

The Sun is shy but I will wait for it

My throat itches and I cough a little.

The rain is playing around us tonight, and it will stay till dawn.

I have pillows but I rest my head on my blanket.

I don't like candies but I chew on this hard coconut bar he gave me.

He bought more than a dozen of it, I hate sweet things that make me thirsty.

I will eat most of it anyway.

My body curved into a C, more like a ball really and I write.

My eyes heavy, half tired and asking for sleep.

What more can we do on continuous days like this?

The Sun is shy but I will wait for it.

Love money not what it buys

Love money not what it buys,

Love people but not what they do.

You can't travel with traitors just because they love adventure too.

Who knows what view they see, you only have your eyes.

They will offer you milk if you love dairy,

But milk is not milk if it is spoiled.

What seems like advice is what ended the beginning of time.

If there is a bridge that takes you to the other end,

Is that side truly where you belong?

Love money not what it buys.

I carry with me songs they dislike

Often so strangely, I want to taste something I do not know of.

Like the way I crave for a specific food but cannot name it.

Just like the way they think I can pour everything on paper,

They assume I cannot suffocate because words can hug me.

Yet there are certain lyrics I cannot sing out loud.

These are of all the places my minds revisits as a guest,

Meeting all the versions of people I saw them as.

They showed me that the way I programmed them was an error.

Now, I carry with me the songs they dislike.

And I will sleep inside the maze

It is really a deadly kind of cold we feel these days,

The weather is slowly changing and the seasons quite dramatic,

Yet I twist and turn my silicon ice mould and pour espresso in a cup.

A shot of sugar and two tablespoons of sweet cream.

Some ramen with extra red sauce as if I could handle the spice.

Tell me when you are drowning more than you could in an ocean and still be calm, what do you call it?

Is this what insanity do to you? Or is it the sane part that stops you from thinking?

For once you do, it's like untangling what is keeping everything tightly in.

I see a forest but I choose to be inside this maze,

There are things we need to take care of before we find freedom and I choose to sleep inside the maze.

Locks and a key

When I was young, I believed that having to meet and greet pain was why I was awarded a gift.

What could be more devastating? That I was wrong, or that, it was the greatest part?

If it's like Frost saying that *I have miles to go before I sleep,*

I hope I fall down and dirty my hands on the mud I fall in.

There are Lotuses starting to grow on land,

And Loctuses starting to heal the waters.

Homes to build and souls to bless,

But Locks and a key cannot do much.

The price to pay for writing was writing.

To the land where blue grass grow

Pack some comfortable clothes and wear rain boots,

There is a place where a cocoon transforming into a butterfly isn't the final evolution.

Horses will not let you ride on them, but it will take you to the meadow where you can feed yourselves.

 Hot air balloons for homes and eyes that moves like vehicles.

You like forms of art like dance and theatre but this is a place art wants to be,

We weren't born to stay forever here and this is why our souls ache.

I will tell you again, wear your rain boots-

It's to the land where blue grass grow.

How we lose before we love

There is irony in most parts that surrounds life.

The most amusingly ironic of it all is how lovers part before they meet.

By the sea shore one waits, while the other on the hill.

You send letters but it comes back to you, you missed the address.

You lose tiny fragments of emotions that you never gave away.

Before you search or long for it, it misplaces itself.

How often a times have we lost before we loved?

To the person who found my letter

I watch a lot of television and this is how I start to dream.

I believe in silly innocent things, it's good for the soul.

To be graced with foolishness might be the strength that gives birth to my weaknesses.

One pleasant afternoon I pleaded Papa to buy me a gas balloon.

It wasn't a fancy cartoon design, but a daring dark red.

I tore a page from my notebook and I wrote a hell lot of what I do not remember.

I wished it on my note to please write back to me, forgetting to mention the return address.

Today, I am twenty three and each time I see a gas balloon fly away,

I have the urge to jump and run and chase it.

To the person who found my letter, maybe none did,

I believe still, that you prayed that I keep writing.

The power we hold

You can love someone and not accept some things they do,

Nobody's hands are clean, we are all tainted.

You cannot support crimes and tell people about righteousness.

You cannot say you love a criminal for his deeds.

Do not wash away love like that.

We can choose to love someone and still hold power over what we do.

Do not be a person who sits there staring at the beauty of the wall just to question yourself later.

Asking, *"what was I trying to do?"* to the mess you built up.

Don't recieve **"nothing"** for an answer.

A woman finds her home

If you put your fingers on my skin and start tracing it,

Make sure you listen to every story my body has to say.

I am not cold as ice, I am made of glass and if you break me,

The hurt is not mine, the wound is yours to carry.

When you find your blood all over my being,

You will miss how you touched me gently in the beginning.

Because a woman finds her home not anywhere but in her.

And if you wreck that, you will built it with your flesh.

All the ways men bend not to break

To feel is a part of life we should call, celebration.

Therefore, I say *homesick*. *Homesick* in ways we never assumed.

In how many ways are you *homesick?* How many places and how many spaces?

How many bullets have you dodged so far?

The ways in which you folded not to lay straight your emotions,

I have been angry for a long time now, nauseous because we are allowed to but, men cannot be *homesick*.

They too look for places with shelter and we offer not none, but more damage.

In hundreds of ways, men bend not to break and never felt at home here on Earth.

We live where we choose to

We walk to reach a destination. It doesn't always have to be somewhere.

Somedays we roam, then we get lost but we do find a way.

If we want to grow, we have to experience.

To close the wound, first there is pain to be felt.

To cherish life, we have to mourn as well.

To have a home to stay we have to decide,

How hard are we willing to toil our hands,

Let our bodies ache and carry with our backs.

We live where we choose to settle.

The power my poems cannot hold

We are here but for a short while, I say.

These are the things I cannot justify in my poems.

We cannot fully ever express what a life can do.

For how can we say how many drops of water makes the ocean,

How I cannot string them together and send it to the moon.

We don't remember what we do here today,

But when your souls decides to part with your body,

The rest of us who see you lifeless terribly pictures every memory.

And that is the power my poems cannot hold.

- This is for everyone we lost but still remains in us.

What I saw at the evening service

Probably a ten year old who can recall more than she should,

Standing alone up there on stage, talking about you Father.

I was older than her but I did not understand it well.

Why is it that when we are young we love you sincerely even though we do not know what grace means?

Is this the miracle of innocence you wanted to protect?

My cousin was three years younger than me, sleeping on aunt's lap.

I wanted to as well, but I was scared of mother but more so of how you see me.

On a cozy evening, I was at chruch and I was the little girl who loved you at hundred percent without doubts.

I now understand why You wanted to desperately save us.

Kü Kangki nai apur

Saka kodang ni apüdak, alima sentsüwangshi ni maki nü.

Saka nai küdang ashi, "Nai junga merangoko, Nü Kangki kü nem aküjang"

www.ingramcontent.com/pod-product-compliance
Lightning Source LLC
LaVergne TN
LVHW050424160726
843469LV00041B/1218